San Francisco

Beautiful

San Francisco

Featuring California Photographers

Text by Lee Foster

Second Printing August, 1978

Published by Beautiful America Publishing Company
4720 S.W. Washington, Beaverton, Oregon 97005
Robert D. Shangle, Publisher

ISBN Number 0-915796-18-X (Paperback)
ISBN Number 0-915796-19-8 (Hard Bound)

BEAUTIFUL AMERICA PUBLISHING COMPANY
CURRENT BOOKS

Utah, Alaska, Hawaii, Arizona, Montana, Michigan,
Colorado, Washington, California, Northern California,
Oregon (Volume II), San Francisco, British Columbia,
California Missions, Western Impressions, Lewis & Clark Country

FORTHCOMING BOOKS

Massachusetts, Southern California, Pennsylvania,
Minnesota, Wisconsin, Maryland, Kentucky,
Georgia, Florida, Illinois, Texas, Ohio

CALENDARS

Texas, Hawaii, Illinois, Florida, Oregon, Colorado, California, New York
Michigan, Washington, Western America, Beautiful America

Send for complete catalog, 50ᶜ

Beautiful America Publishing Company
4720 S.W. Washington, Beaverton, Oregon 97005

CREDITS

Lithography by Fremont Litho Inc., Fremont, California

PHOTO CREDITS

SANDOR BALATONI: Pages 12, 13; pages 16, 17; page 29; page 36; page 41, page 55

PAT DALLAS: Page 56, top

CHARLES PENTICOFF: Page 25; page 28, top; page 32, 33; page 37, top; page 54, top; page 57; page 64, 65

NORMAN PRINCE: Page 52, top

R.W. DIMOND: Pages 48, 49

REV. LOUIS J. RUBELLO: Page 43, top; page 50, bottom; page 52, bottom

TOM TRACY: Page 11, top; page 18; page 20, bottom; page 42; pages 44, 45; page 47; page 50, top

GERALD FRENCH: Page 9, page 25, bottom; page 60

TOM MYERS: Page 40, bottom; page 46, top

WESTERN PHOTO GROUP: Page 10, top and bottom; page 11, bottom; page 14, bottom; page 15; page 19, top and bottom; page 20, top; page 22, top; page 23; page 24, top; page 28, bottom; page 37, bottom; page 40, top; page 43, bottom; page 46, bottom; page 53, top and bottom; page 54, bottom; page 60, top and bottom; page 69, top; page 72, top

LEE FOSTER: Page 14, top; page 56, bottom, page 72, bottom

FRED FELDER: Page 22, bottom

CONTENTS

Introduction

A northern Californian of long standing will sometimes make a conversational reference to "the City". The term will be couched in a deferential, respectful tone. A non-Californian hearing this may wonder if the speaker means Sacramento, Oakland, Berkeley, Palo Alto, or some other place.

But no, "the City is unmistakably San Francisco. The code word and its connotations are immediately understood by a northern Californian: San Francisco has no equal. Other towns may excel it in limited ways; none can match it as a place where urban civilization and culture have achieved an exhilarating level of sophistication.

And what is San Francisco.?

It is everybody's favorite city. This is both a subjective impression and an objective fact. Public-opinion polls have indicated that San Francisco is one of the most visited United States cities, not only by Americans and their proximate neighbors, the Canadians, but by visitors from abroad such as the Japanese, who arrive here some 200,000 strong each year. Those who came here share a conviction that the good life flourishes in San Francisco, a premise that certainly holds true when the city's fine hotels, restaurants, and shops are taken into account. But the community's real assets are less easily identifiable in a specific way. They include, of course, its matchless physical setting and the man-made things, like the Golden Gate Bridge and the cable cars, that have become an integral part of that setting. But perhaps the city's most solid asset is something very immaterial — and that would be its atmosphere of personal freedom.

San Francisco is a city in love with its past. No other American city contemplates its own history with such passionate and narcissistic intensity. But San Francisco may be excused such self-absorption. No other city in the United States has a past marked with such violent and legendary events as its beginnings during the Gold Rush and its (temporary) ending, the earthquake and fire of 1906.

The city's people represent an extraordinary ethnic diveristy. The populace is a composite of hyphenated Americans who tend to celebrate rather than supress their roots. It was fitting that the visionaries who created the United Nations in 1945 happened to do so in the city of unmeltable ethnics.

San Francisco is sometimes saluted for its civilized traditions, but it also offers an ambience of choice, an opportunity for lifestyle exploration, architectural daring, culinary novelty — in short, the search for new answers in all areas of human activity.

All of the various aspects of San Francisco outlined here will be explored in the five essays that follow, with the hope that they will contain something of value for the on-the-spot visitor, in addition to observations that the armchair admirer can savor.

— Lee Foster

Everybody's Favorite City

The taxi driver in Mazatlan asks where I'm from, and I reply, "San Francisco." His face lights up, "Ah, what a beautiful city!" Then he confides that he hasn't been there, but somehow he knows. While conversing with a lady in Paris, I mention that I am from San Francisco, and she responds, "Now that's the American city I'd like to see." A friend in Minneapolis envies me for living here because, she says, "There's so much happening out there."

While most people espouse the merits of their familiar setting, it is surprising how many rank San Francisco as their next favorite place. The magnetism of these 47 square miles on the tip of a peninsula is astonishing. Each year some 2.9 million visitors pass through the city, making their care and feeding the largest local industry. Mobile young people, after finishing college, crowd in with the 685,000 residents, creating keen competition for jobs in professional fields.

When then-mayor Joseph Alioto signed ordinance 307-09 on October 29, 1969, conferring the title, "Official Song of the City and County of San Francisco", on *I Left My Heart in San Francisco,* while Tony Bennett crooned amidst a backdrop of cable cars, the mayor was acknowledging the satisfying fantasy that the song's lyrics project, even if their repetition sometimes seems cloying to a native. Cable cars, hills, fog, and bay are ingredients in the San Francisco recipe. The city has also inspired numerous other songs. In 1914 you might have heard the gushy lyrics of Sidney Carter's *At the Panama Pacific Fair:*

> "Oh, San Francisco, you're a golden nugget!
> Good old San Francisco, I want to kiss and hug it!"

More recently, in 1967, a youth crusade followed the advice in the song *San Francisco* that you go there and, "Be sure to wear a flower in your hair."

An obvious San Francisco trademark is, without doubt, the cable car, a charming and paradoxical conveyance. Cable cars appear improbable, yet they are an efficient means for carrying people up steep hills. Other arrangements, requiring steel or rubber tires, would polish the surface of the street or rail until, with the assist of lubricating rains, the surface would be treacherous. The cable cars appear antiquated, yet how could they be improved?" And who would want to? They are a favorite means of transportation for the visitor, an outing in themselves, yet they are also the everyday travel of the San Franciscan. By comparison, what other city's mass transit system is enjoyed for the pleasure of the trip alone?

The Cable Car Barn and Museum, Washington and Mason streets, presents the history of these charmers and, amazingly enough, lets you gaze closeup at the innards of the system, a 750 horsepower engine turning massive steel wheels and thick cables that can pull at one time a maximum of 31 cars, each weighing 6 tons, at a speed of 9½ miles per hour, up a 21-per-cent grade. The 127 miles of track in the 1880s have been reduced to merely 10½ miles today.

Continued on page 26

8

(Previous Page:) In this photograph the fantastic Hyatt Regency Hotel (center), and the traditional Ferry Building (foreground), depict only one example of a recurring San Francisco motif — the old contrasting with the new.

(Above:) Small fishing boats rest at anchor (foreground), in front of some of the famous seafood restaurants along Fisherman's Wharf.

(Below:) A lovely setting, the Garden Court at the Palace Hotel provides an opulent backdrop for those who enjoy elegant dining. The hotel was built with the silver mining millions of William Ralston.

(Above:) Visitors to the Maritime Museum (at the foot of Hyde Street), will find an interesting assembly of historic ships. The C. A. Thayer, a lumber schooner (right), and the small flat, Alma (left), the last remaining scow from the 19th century are two in the collection. (Below:) On one of San Francisco's balmy days, visitors take time to tour the Japan Center. In the background is the Peace Pagoda.

(Previous Two Pages:) Clouds float lazily in the sky and the Golden Gate Bridge stretches in the foreground in this vista of San Francisco.

(Above:) For over a hundred years San Franciscans have been clinging to cable cars that climb the steep grades. Because of the steep hills, this form of transportation remains almost as efficient as it is picturesque.

(Below:) Shoppers browse in an outdoor flower stall in San Francisco's busy downtown shopping area.

(Opposite Page:) The steeples of Saints Peter and Paul church, framed by the natural beauty of trees and flowering shrubs, rises solemnly over the greenery of Washington Square.

(Previous Two Pages:) The North Beach area, traditionally Chinese and Italian neighborhoods, has played an important role in San Francisco's colorful past. The Coit Tower, brightly illuminated, dominates the scene (upper right).

(Below:) The atrium of the Hyatt Regency Hotel presents the spectator with a fascinating display of 17 tiers of hotel rooms.

(Opposite Page, Above:) A lacy glass confection remaining from the Victorian past, Golden Gate Park's Conservatory is still used to display hothouse flowers and shrubs.

(Opposite Page, Below:) Since "the Rock" was opened for tours by the National Park Service, the famous penal institution on Alcatraz Island has become one of the most frequently visited landmarks in San Francisco. Over two million visitors have seen the now empty prison since it was opened to the public.

(Above:) From the vantage point of Sausalito across the Bay, the San Francisco skyline forms an impressive backdrop for the peaceful waters.
(Below:) Early morning strollers experience a pleasant interlude and enjoy the sunshine in Golden Gate Park.
(Opposite Page:) The new Market Street has retained some of the flavor of its past in the ornate clock with street lamps in the foreground, left. The Bay Area Transit System (BART) speeds along below ground but electric trolleys still continue to operate.

(Above:) A gull basks lazily in the day's last rays of the sun in Aquatic Park.

(Below:) In the new skyline of San Francisco, the Transamerica Building, the thin pyramid in the center of the photograph, is one of the most unusual. Also prominent is the Bank of America Building, the 52-story monolith with bay windows.

(This Page:) These four beautiful Victorian houses are good examples of the many well-kept 18th century style homes still remaining from San Francisco's earlier days.

(This Page and Opposite Page:) Varying moods of the Bay Bridge are shown here, including one with a rainbow shimmering over the tranquil waters.

At the cable car turnaround on Powell you can see Hallidie Plaza, named after this pioneer inventor. It's an appropriate place to board the 20th-century extension of his mass transit vision, the BART (Bay Area Rapid Transit).

When man has altered the environment of San Francisco, controversy has usually accompanied the result. However, there is near universal agreement on the merits of one creation, the Golden Gate Bridge, the most photographed work of man on the earth. In a society whose monuments are secular, the Golden Gate Bridge ranks high and has no peer among bridges. Completed in 1937 under the direction of engineer Joseph Strauss, the bridge is open to walkers daily from sunrise to sunset. Painted international orange, a color that offsets favorably the coastal flora of Marin County hillsides to the north, the bridge spans a narrow waterway of powerful inrushing and outgoing tides where the Sacramento-San Joaquin River systems drain into the sea.

To the south extends the Bay Bridge, a grey 8¼-mile, work-a-day mass of steel that connects the East Bay with San Francisco. The Bay Bridge is longer and less glamorous than the Golden Gate, but more vital to the commercial life of the city.

San Francisco pleases partly because of its manageable size. In a short time you feel that you can know it, though not begin to exhaust it. Some cities sprawl even if small, such as Phoenix, and others are unfocussed, such as Los Angeles, but San Francisco has a compact, easy-to-get-around-in feeling. And the 40 hills always present a new vista, a varied, seldom-repeated appearance, aided by the changing light and fog. Cable cars, busses, and BART carry people efficiently to their destinations. With the longest street, Geary, measuring only 5 miles, San Francisco is one of America's best walking towns. Mountain-climber types may wish to know that the steepest streets are Filbert between Leavenworth and Hyde, and 22nd between Church and Vicksburg, both with a 31.5 per cent gradient. And the crooked-est street, Lombard between Leavenworth and Hyde, delights those who seek out the picturesque.

San Francisco offers to native and visitor an air of freedom, a chance to think what is unthinkable elsewhere and to live in ways declared outrageous in other parts of the country. San Francisco presents a holiday from conformity, a place to let down, an opportunity to be what you wish, perhaps also to glimpse behavioral arrangements whose time is yet to come.

To some extent this freedom arose because of the city's origin. During the Gold Rush people from all over the world poured in, forming an instant society. The diversity of backgrounds required a tolerance that was by no means complete, but was notable when compared with the uniformity of other societies. And as a port town, San Francisco has always been open to influences from the Orient and elsewhere.

This openness has made the city a lifestyle laboratory where people experiment with ways of living, with relating to each other and to the environment. Often these experiments set trends that become widespread elsewhere. For example, if the national environmental movement could be said to have had a birth, perhaps the most significant single event was the 1962 rejection by San Franciscans of a freeway that would have cut people off from the waterfront between the Ferry Building and the Golden Gate. You can still see this freeway literally hanging in the air where it was stopped along the Embarcadero.

Only in San Francisco could you be a vegetarian in the spiritual self-help movement (Est) with a flair for the Oriental (Krishna Consciousness) while working for prosperous underground journalism (Bay Guardian) and living in a commune wharehouse (several south of Market). If the psychic input became overwhelming, you could consult practitioners of the new ''holistic'' medicine, who would try to maximize further your well-being.

San Francisco has always been a place of good living, with lively bars and superb restaurants, an incredible 2,600 in this small area. The variety of restaurants stuns the imagination. At one, you can eat buffalo stew and scan a decor of flotsam-jetsam western Americana. In every category of classic food there are restaurants where *haute cuisine* is a reality. And there are always newcomers who make San Francisco a place of culinary discoveries. Every tenth San Franciscan dreams of his own, perfect restaurant, and goes through life sampling the alternatives, refining the vision.

Hotels of the city have been legendary since 1876 when William Ralston built his white and gold Palace Hotel, Market and Montgomery. Financed with five million uninflated dollars that Ralston amassed as his share of silver in Virginia City, Nevada's famous Comstock Lode, the Palace boasted 800 rooms and a palm court carriage entrance. The hotel's splendor was shattered by the quake and fire of 1906, but was meticulously rebuilt with the palm court transformed into an elegant dining room, the garden court, which should be glimpsed today as a flash of *fin de siècle* grandeur.

Among the new hotels, the Hyatt Regency, 5 Embarcadero Center, is one of the most stunning. Designed to approximate a small San Francisco hill, the outside walls tier inward and the interior rises for a full 17 stories of unencumbered space. Walking into the hotel gives you the feeling of entering a spacious underground city. Between 5 to 8 p.m. on Fridays the entire atrium becomes an impromptu ballroom as bands strike up an end-of-the-week party for hotel guests and work-weary San Franciscans.

Typically of San Francisco, even the grimmer and less presentable sides of the city's life have a vitality and interest for natives and visitors. Who would have guessed a few years ago that the most draconian monument to American penal history, Alcatraz Island, would become the most visited attraction in San Francisco? More than 2.2 million people have paid their $2 at Pier 41 to take the United States Park Service's 2½-hour excursion to the island, touring the ''Hole'', where men stripped naked were forced to live in total darkness for 18-day stretches on metal floors without heat, fortified with a daily diet of bread and water.

In San Francisco you can take a Gray Lines tour highlighting the beautiful, comfortable, and approved sights and then complement this with a Glide Church anti-tour that takes you through ''Third World'' and disadvantaged neighborhoods.

(Above:) Seagulls follow one of the many excursion boats which crisscross San Francisco Bay, here flying over the wake left by the vessel.
(Below:) Union Square provides a pleasant place to enjoy a quiet respite for anyone strolling through the center of the city.
(Opposite Page:) A cable car driver turns the car by hand at the foot of the street, as a potential passengers await their turn to ride.

The City in Love
With Its Past

No American city has a love affair with its past more intense than San Francisco's. This may be narcissism, but of a kind so harmless that no perjorative connotations can be attached to it. The San Franciscan loves his Victorian architecture and wants to show it to you just as an Amsterdammer appreciates his 17th-century canal houses. And the San Franciscan dwells on the instant and accidental founding of the city — the Gold Rush — the way an informed Mexico City resident, showing you through the Museum of Anthropology, will recall the capricious decision to found Tenochtitlan when a priest sighted an eagle with a snake in its claws.

Each of the eras of San Francisco history remains alive today, both as artifacts you can visit and as legend to nourish the imagination, starting with the tranquility of the Spanish-Mexican era from 1776 to the 1840s, then the exhilarating shock of the Gold Rush after 1848, followed by the reflective gentility of the later 19th century, all shattered by the quake and fire of 1906.

The Spanish era of San Francisco's history ccan only be described as bucolic and, in some respects, idyllic. In 1776 Juan Bautista de Anza completed a long trek northward from San Ignacio de Tubac to establish here a presidio and settlement. Following close upon de Anza was the indefatigable Franciscan, Junipero Serra, who founded Mission San Francisco de Asis, his sixth in California. Popularly known as Mission Dolores, after a nearby swamp, the structure at 16th and Dolores still stands, restored but not altered, the oldest unchanged building in San Francisco. Constructed of sun-dried bricks, the walls are four feet thick. Since no nails were available, wooden pegs and rawhide held the building together. The lines of the mission suggest the simplicity and austerity of frontier California at a time when the Declaration of Independence preoccupied the 13 colonies on the east coast of the continent. Don Luis Antonio Arguello, the first Spanish governor of California, lies buried in the small adjacent graveyard. The interior roof remains as it was painted in angular shapes more than 150 years ago by Indians using vegetable colors.

The Spanish-Mexican society of the San Francisco region emphasized immense families, sometimes as many as 20 children, and the arts of horsemanship, with cattle as the important trade item. Boston trading ships landed in California ports to pick up the hides, called ''California banknotes''.

By the 1830s San Francisco and Monterey proved attractive to a few Yankees, who saw the area from whaling or trading ships and decided to settle. Adventurers of other nationalities also stopped and stayed, among them entrepreneur John Sutter, who touched at San Francisco and then pushed inland to the area of Sacramento where he hoped to establish an agricultural empire, naming it New Helvetia after the Latin for his native Switzerland.

The event that was to transform the drowsy sand-duned trading post of San Francisco into an international city occurred at a sawmill that James Marshall was building in 1848 for

John Sutter on the American River, about 110 air miles northeast of the city. Marshall discovered some yellow nuggets in the race below the mill. When it was determined that the material was indeed gold, the story could hardly be suppressed.

Between 1848 and 1852 California was transformed from a pastoral scattering of Spanish-Mexican villages with a population of 15,000 to a restless prospecting region of 250,000. Statehood came in 1850. By 1852 an estimated $200 million in gold had been mined.

In San Francisco you can see remaining from this era a brick fortification called Fort Point immediately below the south anchor of the Golden Gate Bridge. Juan Bautista de Anza first planted a cross here in 1776 and the Spaniards erected a crude stockade by 1794. Today the Civil-War-era fort remains as a prime example of 19th-century United States military architecture. Fittingly in the city dedicated to peaceful St. Francis, the fort never fired a shot in anger.

The Jackson Square Historic District, bounded by Kearney, Washington, Sansome, and Pacific is an interesting cluster of brick buildings from the 1850s-60s. The Hotaling Building at 451 Jackson was once a liquor warehouse. At the Montgomery-Jackson streets corner stands the Lucas Turner & Co. Bank, begun in 1853 by William T. Sherman. Today lawyers, designers, art dealers, and antique dealers occupy the core historic buildings.

Each Jackson Square structure has its story to tell. The Langerman Building at 722 Montgomery, now the law offices of famed attorney Melvin Belli, was built in 1849-50, then rebuilt after a fire. It served first as a tobacco warehouse, became the Melodeon Theater, where entertainer Lotta Crabtree performed, later was an auctioneering site, and then a Turkish bath. The adjacent Genella Building, 728-730 Montgomery, tells more of the story of San Francisco's early diversity. Joseph Genella erected it in 1853-54 for his residence and business in china and glassware. Subsequent activities included a bullion dealership, merchandise brokerage, a Spanish newspaper *(La Voz de Chile)*, and a mining office. Near the corner of Sansome and Clay the *Niantic,* a grounded ship, served as a hotel. Hundreds of abandoned hulls became floating residences and stores during the Gold Rush.

The Wells Fargo Bank History Room, 420 Montgomery, is another instructive stop. There you can view a Concord stagecoach and read the free giveaway, a copy of the 1887 *Tips For Stagecoach Drivers,* which suggests you ''spit on the leeward side'' and ''never shoot on the road as the noise might frighten the horses.'' This small museum contains such monetary curiosities as a $50 octagonal gold slug issued by the United States assay office in 1852. Wells Fargo also tells the story of its antagonist, Black Bart, the most prominent highway robber of 19th-century California. Bart robbed 28 stages singlehandedly, never harming a passenger, leaving mocking doggerel verses at the scene of the crime.

While downtown, catch the California and then the Powell cable cars to Union Square, named after a mass meeting in 1861 when Californians decided to side with the Union. If there is one place in San Francisco where you can see the whole spectrum of humanity pass by, it is Union Square, so seat yourself on a bench for a restful hour in the sun to watch the kaleidoscopic procession of people.

31

(Following Two Pages:) This breathtaking aerial photograph of west San Francisco shows the Bay Bridge, Oakland, and the vista beyond to Mt. Diablo.

After browsing the smart shops of the area, such as Gump's, 250 Post, with its remarkable collection of jade, catch the streetcar on Market to the Civic Center and peruse the large building of Italian Renaissance design, City Hall. Walk through its regal interior and then browse the Public Library opposite. Behind City Hall lies the Opera House-War Memorial, where the Museum of Modern Art sponsors changing shows.

San Francisco's circa 1860-1900 Victorian houses, whether palaces or modest residences, add much to the charm of the city. You can tour one of the most striking and best preserved of these dwellings, the Haas-Lilienthal House, 2007 Franklin, built in 1886. Its gables, bay windows, turret tower, and exuberance of gingerbread make Haas-Lilienthal a classic Queen Anne paralleled in its Victorian accoutrements only by the conservatory greenhouse in Golden Gate Park. The interior still houses much of the original decor, with mahogany walls, marble hearths, and fine tapestries.

The adjacent residential area, known as Pacific Heights, is considered one of San Francisco's choice living areas. Some other prominent Victorians are the Spreckels mansion, 2080 Washington, and the California Historical Society building, 2090 Jackson. The latter is open to visitors and is filled with period furnishings. Streets adjacent to Lafayette Square offer many examples of Victorian architecture. At 1000 California stands the James Flood mansion, built in 1886 by the Comstock-silver-lode millionaire. Today the Flood mansion is the last of the great mansions from the baronial days of the mining and railroad kings. Others in the neighborhood of the Flood mansion were swept away in the fires that followed the quake.

The Great Earthquake and Fire that destroyed San Francisco on April 18, 1906 has had a profound effect on the sensibility as well as physical look of the city. The shaking was not as devastating as the three days of fires, fed by broken natural gas lines and checked only with dynamite because the water mains were destroyed and private wells proved inadequate.

As a result of the quake, with 28,000 buildings and 500 people lost, San Francisco developed a fondness for firemen, whether expressed in Lillie Hitchcock Coit's fire nozzle, Coit Tower (a splendid place to view the city), or in the unusually high pay, comparable to that of policemen, the San Francisco firemen receive.

The quake has always been viewed by San Franciscans with a *carpe diem* irreverence, partly because a repeat performance is inevitable. Lyrics of a song by Charles Field, referring to the Hotaling liquor warehouse in Jackson Square, caught the spirit of the city's response:

> "If, as they say, God spanked the town
> for being over frisky,
>
> why did He burn the churches down
> and spare Hotalings's whiskey?"

The city's wharf area also leans heavily on the nostalgia aroused by its historic buildings. The two wharf complexes on Beach Street, Ghirardelli Square and the Cannery, are a former factories which have acquired a patina of romance over the years. Domingo Ghirardelli's building was a Civil War uniform factory, a woolen works, and eventually a turn-of-the-century candy factory. Today it houses shops and restaurants, as does the Cannery, formerly home of the Del Monte Fruit and Vegetable Cannery.

San Francisco's maritime history has been carefully preserved. At the foot of Hyde Street you can visit the Maritime State Historic Park, which berths five restored ancient boats. *Alma* is an 1891 scow schooner, last of the hundreds of scows that plied San Francisco Bay waters with loads of hay, lumber, bricks, and coal. The three-masted *C.A. Thayer* is a prime example of the soil-powered lumber schooners that worked the coastal lumber trade in the decades before efficient roads. *Wapama* is a steam schooner and *Eureka* a side-wheel ferryboat. Recently the collection expanded to include *Hercules,* a steam tug.

Maritime history comes alive on a Sunday in late May when the *Alma* leads a concourse of vintage sailing boats in a race around the Bay, called the Master Mariners Regatta. Each of the participants, ancient wooden sailing craft that were often working boats, receives its starting gun salute at the beach in front of the St. Francis Yacht Club. Today's race recalls the Master Mariners Regatta of the 1860s, when the competitive crews of lumber schooners and hay scows, after storing up their cabin fever for a year, would engage in a 4th of July race to determine once and for all who was the fastest. This Independence Day Master Mariners Regatta was an event of consequence in San Francisco of the 1860s-70s. Non-sailors often chartered a boat to go out for a look at the race in the middle of the bay. As ballast the charter boats laid in stores of chicken salad sandwiches and kegs of beer.

As the era of the gas guzzler auto comes to an end, the palaces along Van Ness Avenue deifying the American car will become historic legacies. At 901 Van Ness one Earl C. Anthony opened a spacious showroom in 1927 to celebrate his 22nd anniversary as the Packard representative. He brought in the noted architect, Bernard Maybeck, to design cherubim that fly amidst the worm-eaten Florida swamp cypress ceilings and the mammoth Belgian black marble columns. A Gothic archway leads to the ''mechanics salon'' upstairs. British Motors, the current occupant of the building, uses this regal setting to advantage for displaying its Rolls Corniches and Jensen Interceptors.

In 1921 the Don Lee Cadillac dealership at 1000 Van Ness also honored the American car in a palatial showroom with Spanish tile floor, carved hardwood staircases, and bronze coffered ceilings. Out front, smiling bears are seated atop columns. Beside the front door a swarm of cherubim fly up and down the columns. Above the door sit two greater-than-life-size nudes, with 1921 haircuts, holding in their hands two variations of a 1921 Cadillac wheel, one with 8 spokes, the other with 12.

(Opposite Page:) San Francisco's Chinatown is the largest Chinese community outside the Orient. Here the wax museum is outlined with strings of bright lights.

(Above:) With its back to a hill, Sausalito is well protected from the open sea, making the bayside town in Marin County an interesting tourist attraction. Sausalito is located across the Bay north of San Francisco.

(Below:) Shown here is one of several restaurants in Sausalito that have been built on pilings over the water's edge.

The City Gifted By Nature

San Francisco sits on the edge of a peninsula separating the Pacific Ocean from San Francisco Bay, one of the world's great natural harbors. With water on three sides, fog rolling in and out, and 40 hills to present the drama, the experience of San Francisco amounts to an unusual wedding of urban amenities and natural features. Of the city's hills Davidson is the highest and Twin Peaks, the geographic center, commands the most sweeping views.

On many mornings and evenings, especially in summer, a heavy blanket of fog pushes across the city, triggering a dazzling interplay of light and shadow. The cool damp air of the fog holds San Francisco's temperature to a comfortable mean of 57 degrees with only moderate variations. In a year of normal rainfall about 21 inches drop on the city between November and April. The westerly winds that propel sailboats around the bay on sunny afternoons also keep San Francisco relatively free of smog, even in the warmest month, September.

Even within the city the appreciator of wild nature can find some satisfaction. Consider the Mycological Society, which gathers at 9 a.m. each Sunday morning in winter near the Rodin fountain at the Palace of the Legion of Honor and makes a foray into the wild Land's End area looking for mushrooms. Members and other persons who care to join them sometimes see the rare San Francisco garter snake, an endangered species, but mushrooms are the main quarry. The wild mushrooms in the area are prolific, nurtured by the wet fog and bright sun. Shaggy manes, agaricus rodmanii, parasols, and various boletus are all eagerly sought and gathered in great numbers by the mycophagists, or mushroom eaters, within the ranks. The poisonous *Amanitas pantherina* and *muscaria* are merely observed. Each November the Academy of Sciences in Golden Gate Park hosts a mushroom fair that displays hundreds of wild mushrooms from the San Francisco region. These autumn gatherings are lavish and colorful, both as to mushrooms and their admirers. A very-San Francisco event, indeed.

Another species of nature-lover, genus San Francisco, can be observed at the foot of Hyde Street, headquarters of the Dolphin Club, an association founded by a half dozen German sport enthusiasts in 1877. The Dolphins specialize in swimming the chilly bay waters. You can usually see them streaking across the cove in front of Aquatic Park. On more ambitious days they swim the Golden Gate itself, fighting not only the chill but the swift currents.

When looking at San Francisco today, it is difficult to imagine that in the 19th century much of the western half was a shifting sand dune that some expert landscapists such as Frederick Law Olmsted, despaired of taming. Coastal strand plant communities in relatively undisturbed states can be found on the hillsides in the south part of Sutro Heights Park, on dunes around Baker Beach, and on hillsides between Lincoln Boulevard and the beach west of the Golden Gate. In the spring these areas show dozens of native wildflowers of every shape and color, including Indian paint brush, yellow sand verbena, California poppy, seaside daisy, wild buckwheat, beach lupine, yarrow, and yellow bush lupine.

Because so much of San Francisco in 1868 was an uninhabited sand dune region, the city fathers showed some foresight when they set aside 800,000 uninflated dollars for the purchase and development of 1017 acres to be known as Golden Gate Park. Like the great hotels and the opera house, the park was both a gesture to the future and a legacy, an index of the confidence that San Franciscans had in the city's growth and destiny, a sense that the city would later need the civilizing and recreational opportunities afforded by a major park.

The man who transformed Golden Gate Park, then about 730 acres of dunes and 270 acres of arable land scattered with live oaks, was a small stocky Scotsman, born in Stirling in 1846, who migrated to California in 1870. In 1887 the park commission appointed this man, John McLaren, as park superintendent, a post he held for an incredible 59 years until his death in 1943.

McLaren's first task was to continue his predecessors' efforts at anchoring the dunes with a mixture of ice plant, northern European beach grass, and the tea tree from Australia. One year he asked for and received from the park commission the street sweepings of San Francisco as his birthday present. With this ample supply of horse manure assured, he built the ground turf that allowed later impressive plantings of trees and meadows. McLaren, who liked to be addressed with the simple term, ''boss gardener'', planted more than 5,000 different kinds of shrubs, flowers, and trees in the park. He used the Monterey Cypress to good advantage at the west end where it thrives in the sea winds. In the quieter recesses of the park he favored the Australian eucalyptus, with its dappled bark and heady gum smell. The climate was his ally in the rose garden, where roses bloom even in December.

To many observers Golden Gate Park is the most elegant urban park in the country, with resources varied enough to fulfill its original written mandate that the park was ''primarily intended to provide the best practical means for healthful recreation for people of all classes.''

Along Kennedy Drive, stop to admire the Victorian conservatory, a lacy glass confection covering hothouse begonias and tropical plants, with a greeting card of flowers on the front lawns.

You can relax over tea at the Japanese Tea Garden, especially enjoyable at April cherry blossom time. Nearby are the art holdings of the De Young Memorial Museum and the natural history displays of the California Academy of Sciences. At the Steinhardt Aquarium you can see a golden garibaldi fish that grows up to 14 inches off the California coast. Summer concerts in the music concourse are presented free on Sunday afternoons.

The famous Strybing Arboretum is almost a park within a park, with its acres of labeled trees and shrubs. Of special interest is the California native plant section, including a complete conifer walk, a short cut to learning the identity of conifers in the most coniferous state.

You will look in vain for a ''Keep Off The Grass'' sign. John McLaren stressed that the park should be used, including its 11 lakes, 2 stadiums, 27 miles of footpaths, and 16 miles of bridle paths. One of the two moribund windmills at the west end of the park will eventually be restored.

Continued on page 58

(Above:) A huge sign welcomes tourists to one of San Francisco's most famous attractions, Fisherman's Wharf — a perfect place for sight-seeing, shopping, and dining.

(Below:) The Italian community has contributed several fine examples to the list of San Francisco's famous restaurants, as attested to by some of the Italian names shown on these signs along Fisherman's Wharf.

(Opposite Page:) Two bright stars in the brilliantly lit San Francisco nighttime skyline are the Transamerica Building pyramid and the Bank of America Building.

(Below:) Surrounded by a sea of cars, Candlestick Park is obviously popular, with a full-capacity crowd here. The huge stadium is located in the southeast corner of San Francisco.

(Opposite Page, Above:) Sunrise over San Francisco is an event well worth getting up early to witness, as this photograph amply illustrates.

(Opposite Page, Below:) The Japanese Tea Garden in Golden Gate Park is a most charming example of Japanese style landscaping. Tea ceremonies and bonsai enhance the exotic beauty of the park.

(Following Two Pages:) First rays of the morning sun silhouette the San Francisco skyline beneath the Bay Bridge.

(Opposite Page, Above:) Dining out continues to be one important facet of the San Francisco lifestyle, and the list of famous restaurants is impressive. At Sam's in Tiburon, the gin fizz is the most popular drink.

(Opposite Page, Below, and This Page:) Called the "most crooked street in the world", Lombard weaves its way between Hyde and Leavenworth Streets, with clusters of flowers and shrubs outlining its curves.

(Following Two Pages:) San Francisco's famous skyline is shown here with the Bay Bridge on one side and Sausalito on the other side. This view was taken looking over Richardson's Bay.

(Opposite Page, Above:) This replica of Sir Francis Drake's ship, the Golden Hinde *recently sailed from England to San Francisco. The trip retraced a 16th century voyage, during which Drake stopped briefly in the area to take on water, supplies, and repair the ship.*
(Opposite Page, Below:) Much of the waterfront skyline shown here is built on land reclaimed from the Bay by gradual filling.
(Below:) Ghirardelli and the Cannery are former chocolate and fish factoriees at Fisherman's Wharf which have been converted into space for shops and restaurants. Here the lights of Ghirardelli reflect on part of the Bay.

(Above:) Crossing the Golden Gate Bridge by car or truck, the view is splendid, but the trip is even better for pedestrians, who can stop and take an unhurried look at the surrounding beauty.

(Below:) the Palace of Fine Arts is a legacy to San Franciscans, left over from the Panama Pacific Exposition of 1915.

(Above:) The San Francisco de Asis Mission, the sixth one built by Franciscans in California, is also known as Mission Dolores. Spanish influence on architecture and customs has always been considerable, even in the early years, before San Francisco became a major city. (Below:) City Hall was rebuilt after the 1906 earthquake, as was most of downtown San Francisco.

(Above:) This exciting aerial view of San Francisco encompasses the Golden Gate Bridge and some of the hills surrounding the Bay. To the north are the Marin County hills.

(Below:) The War Memorial Opera House at the Civic Center is the location of the Museum of Modern Art, which hosts changing exhibits of art, and its own permanent collection.

(Opposite Page:) Reflected in the water is the elegant Palace of Fine Arts. The gracefully designed building remains from the Panama Pacific Exposition of 1915.

(Above:) A common sight in the western port of San Francisco is fog. Here blue sky and sunshine contrast with the low-lying mist hovering over clustered houses.

(Below:) Perhaps the best view of one of the most impressive skylines to be found anywhere in the world can be obtained from aboard a boat. Passengers on incoming or outgoing ships get a special treat as they pass below the Golden Gate Bridge.

(Opposite Page:) Like graceful birds in flight, small sailing vessels ride the bay beneath the Golden Gate bridge. Fog in the Bay Area always brings with it a symphony of foghorns as boats glide through its heavy mantle.

The nature lover in San Francisco also owes a thank you for the inadvetent preservation occasioned by the presence of the United States Army, whose 1,400-acre Presidio, largest military post in a United States city, now gives San Francisco a huge green breathing space and playground.

As if to augment John McLaren's dream, the parks of San Francisco are expanding rather than contracting. Indeed, the appreciation of nature and a deliberate effort to arrest any encroachment on nature characterize the people of Marin County and San Francisco. The newest development is the creation of a 34,000-acre Golden Gate National Recreation Area to embrace the many parklands in the immediate San Francisco-and-north region. Starting at the southwest end of San Francisco, this park wraps a 10-mile ribbon of greenery and sand around the western and northern shores of the city.

Beginning at the southwest are the Fort Funston dunes, fortunately held by the military until they had no more strategic value and the public had the will and resources to acquire them. Hang gliding enthusiasts favor Funston as the best west coast site for catching the winds that blow landward, bounce off the cliffs, and shoot up, carrying hang gliders aloft for minutes or hours as the pilot chooses, drifting up and down the beaches, confident that in any emergency a gentle landing could be made on the sand and iceplant terrain.

Stretching northward is the long Ocean Beach. At the end stands the venerable Cliff House and its jutting rocks, home for cormorants and barking sea lions, though misnamed Seal Rock. After you glance at the ghostly outline of the once fashionable saltwater Sutro Baths adjacent to the Cliff House, step into the building for a look at a unique store, San Franciscana, which specializes in books and images about the city, past and present. On the walls you can see huge posters showing what the Sutro Baths were like when they were flourishing. For $2 you can select a photograph made from an original negative showing San Francisco in he 1890s or perhaps after the quake of 1906. Here's the place to get postcards of turn-of-the-century bathing beauties who were rash enough to show their ankles or even more. Between Land's End and the bridge is Baker Beach, another fine stretch for surf fishing, strolling, wading, and hiking. Picnickers favor protected places in the adjacent cypress forests.

The most recently added attraction for nature lovers in San Francisco is the Golden Gate Promenade, a newly-opened 3½-mile stretch of beach between Fisherman's Wharf and the Golden Gate. As this area becomes cleared and landscaped in future years, it will emerge as one of the great urban walks in the world. More of a hike than a promenade, the path gives you a good sense of the bay, beach, islands, and sailboats. Beachcombers delight in the debris that the sea turns up here. To make this walk, begin with the promenade signs at the wharf or at Marina Green.

The promenade offers your best opportunity in the city to see the bird life that thrives on and around San Francisco Bay. Cormorants are abundant during the spring and can be seen diving for small fish. Terns also dive from the air and grab their prey while scarcely losing a wingbeat. Occasionally brown pelicans can be seen skimming over the waters only a few inches above the waves. Blackbirds, killdeer, and sanderlings are abundant along the walk.

San Francisco is one of the few cities whose outlying parts are accessible only by boat. Alcatraz Island has some natural features of note (it was named after the pelican), but larger Angel Island, reached by ferryboat from Pier 43, offers more for the nature enthusiast. On Angel Island you can see a wide range of California native plants while walking, picnicking, or bicycling. This greenery is, like the Presidio, an unplanned gift from the military. At times past, Angel Island served as a kitchen garden for the Alcatraz prison, a backup area for our soldiers in wartime, and an immigration station. In the 1970s Angel Island has also been an example of nature gone askew when the balance was upset by the exclusion of predators. The deer population exploded and depleted the vegetation until park authorities took steps to thin the herd to manageable numbers. Today Angel Island approximates the natural setting that Juan Manuel de Ayala saw when he sailed the first boat through the Golden Gate in 1775. He chose to land his *San Carlos* at Angel Island.

(Above:) One of the many places in San Francisco to see interesting art exhibits, the Palace of the Legion of Honor is a showpiece in itself. Major traveling art exhibitions can be seen here, and the building also houses its own art and antique collection of mainly French pieces.

(Opposite Page, Above:) Parks along the northwest edge of the city, now part of the Golden Gate National Recreation Area, offer superb views of the Golden Gate.

(Opposite Page, Below:) A close-up view of the stately columns of the Palace of the Legion of Honor gives a good view of the design of the architecture.

The City of
Unmeltable Ethnics

If the San Francisco native or visitor happens to turn an FM radio dial to Ken and Karla Carey's special station, KBRG (105.3), on a weekday evening from 9:30-11, the program will be, surprisingly, in Chinese. If that same radio listener dialed the station at 6-8 p.m. on a weekday, he would find the braodcast in Italian. During most of the day the programs are in Spanish. But Wednesday to Friday evening, 8:30-9:30, there is Japanese.

And that is only the beginning. In the course of a week KBRG broadcasts an hour or more in Arabic, Armenian, Indian, Estonian, French, German, Greek, Hungarian, Irish, Korean, Polish, Portugese, Russian, Serbian, and Tagalog. The existence of this radio station, and the market for it, reveals San Francisco's thoroughly international ethnic mix.

A hyphenated American has never had to apologize for his ethnicity in San Francisco, the city composed of ethnics. Though it has become popular in the last decade throughout the country to embrace one's national origins, it has always been the custom to do so in San Francisco. Those without an ethnic specialty in San Francisco often tend to follow one of the lifestyle innovations that differentiate in a manner more radical than ethnic origin.

San Francisco's Chinatown, largest Chinese community outside the orient, began in the 1850s when Chinese fled natural disaster and political upheaval in the south China Kwangtung Province and city of Canton. Today about one in ten San Franciscans is of Chinese origin. In the 1860s and 70s thousands of Chinese workers came to construct the Central Pacific Railroad. In the past decade Chinatown has been rejuvenated by 40,000 immigrants from Hong Kong and Taiwan, filling a gap left when Chinese moved out of the city or to some other area, such as the prosperous Richmond, now the home of about 20 per cent of San Francisco's 75,000 Chinese. The opening up of trade with mainland China in recent years has also brought renewed vitality to Chinatown.

Portsmouth Square is the focus for the visitor and for the 35,000 Chinese living in the immediate area. In the early morning tai chi chuan practitioners do exercises there. Later in the day children and older adults enjoy the sun of the park, feed the pigeons, and play Chinese chess. To know Chinatown you must walk it, beginning with Portsmouth Square, once the focus of San Francisco when the Bay waterline came nearly to the area. Here California pioneer Sam Brannan made an historic announcement that gold had been discovered, showing skeptics a few nuggets, which promptly turned San Francisco into a ghost town.

In 1880 Scots writer Robert Louis Stevenson mused away his time here, just as hundreds of San Franciscans do every day. A stone bridge links Portsmouth Square with the Chinese Culture Foundation, on the third floor of the Holiday Inn hotel building. The foundation sponsors interpretive exhibits about Chinese life in America. Other displays can be seen at the Chinese Historical Museum, 17 Adler Place, off 1140 Grand.

The food markets, especially on Stockton between Washington and Broadway, exhibit an awesome variety of Chinese vegetables, such as bok choi and chard, or meat animals, including ducks and pigeons. The numerous fat ducks hanging raw or cooked and the bags of paper-thin dried fish are two unusual sights for the occidental, but on Stockton you may even see a butcher carve up a turtle.

Chinatown has many special places to browse, among them Old Chinatown Lane, off 868 Washington, which contains some of the few buildings in the area that survived the fires after the 1906 quake. The lane was noted for its proliferation of gambling and opium establishments. The Mandarin Co., 64 Wentworth, carries records, cassettes, and the original instruments used to create Chinese music. Three temples on Waverly Place are open for the meditator who seeks a quiet respite from the city. High quality jade and ivory carvings can be examined at Chinese Arts and Crafts, 823 Grant, and Jade Empire, 742 Grant. The Mow Lee grocery at 774 Commerical, in business since 1856, is the oldest grocery in Chinatown.

An infusion of goods and thinking from mainland China has revitalized Chinatown in the last decade. The Man Fung China Trading Co., 1301 Stockton, stocks all-mainland wares, ranging from dried mushrooms to down jackets, lacquerware to landscapes hand-painted on egg shells. The New China Bookstore, 642 Pacific, carries extensive literature portraying the vision of the People's Republic.

Chinese New Year, late January-early February, is a festive time for all San Franciscans. Firecrackers, a Chinese invention, turn the metal and stone canyons of the city into a deafening battleground. Children of all ages wait along the parade route for a glimpse at the huge dragon of the Chinese New Year Parade, a lavish event complete with marching band and a Miss Chinatown U.S.A. The Chinese use a sequential series of animals to identify the years. After the 1977 Year of the Serpent come years for the horse, ram, monkey, rooster, dog, boar, rat, ox, tiger, hare, and dragon.

With recent mayors bearing the names Moscone and Alioto, it should be no surprise that San Francisco has a substantial Italian colony, about 150,000 residents of Italian descent, focussed historically in the North Beach area but now diffused throughout the city. In October the Italians celebrate Columbus' discovery of America with a re-enactment of the event, a Columbus Day Parade, and the blessing of the fleet at Fisherman's Wharf. At the Aquatic Park courts, Van Ness and North Point, you can sometimes see bocce ball played. San Francisco is one of the few cities in the United States where Italians continue this lawn bowling tradition, said to have begun with the Romans in the time of the Caesars.

The center of Italian activity in San Francisco is Washington Square in North Beach. From a window table of the Washington Square Bar and Grill, 1707 Powell, you can look over Little Italy. Another typical Italian restaurant is the Fior d'Italia, 621 Union, directly on the square. This establishment has been operated continuously since 1886, making it the oldest Italian restaurant in the city. During all those years it has also been in the same family, the Armido Marianetti clan.

The Mexican-Americans of the Mission District have a startling new art form to show visitors, the wall mural, reminiscent of what a traveler might see in the works of Diego Rivera or Clement Orozco in Mexico. At the Mexican Museum, 15th and Folsom, take in

63

the current show and pick up a free walking map of the murals, four of which are especially prominent. They are located at the minipark on 24th a half block east of Bryant, at 2922 Mission, at the BART station on 24th and Mission, and at 24th and Van Ness. These murals take as their theme the cycle of life, fertility and farming, latin America, and the struggle of work. A fifth mural with an entirely different style and theme is Mike Rios' cartoon creation about people and their legal problems, on the San Francisco Legal Assistance Building, 23rd and Folsom.

The main Mexican-American celebrations in San Francisco are Cinco de Mayo, recalling every May 5 the 1862 victory over the French at the Battle of Puebla; and the 16th of September, Mexican Independence Day, a week of parades, dances, and special festivities, including at City Hall the famous "El Grito de Dolores", a re-enactment of Miguel Hidalgo's historic yell announcing independence from Spain in 1810.

Japanese in San Francisco focus their ethnic energies every April for the Cherry Blossom Festival, celebrated at the five-acre Japan Center, Post and Buchanan. Adjacent Japantown, (called Nihonmachi), especially the Buchanan Street pedestrian mall, is a good browsing place any time, complete with its styliized torii (gates), flowering cherry and plum trees, kimono store, fountains, benches, and a ribbon of bricks forming a Japanese dry stream.

The Japan Center includes the Miyako Hotel, a peace pagoda, and numerous shops and restaurants. The shops specialize in ceramics, lacquerware, cameras, electronics, art objects, clothing, and flower arranging. At the Kame Sushi Bar you can eat the raw fish so prized in Japan.

During the Cherry Blossom Festival you can listen to folk songs, watch dancing, even hear thunderous taiko (Japanese drum) concerts. On hand are masters of the various Japanese martial arts of judo, akido, kendo, kempo, taido, and karate. Displays present Japanese art, calligraphy, silk screens, dolls, bonsai, pottery, flower arranging, classical koto music, and the tea ceremony.

The Irish of San Francisco celebrate St. Patrick's Day on March 17 with all other nationals prepared to switch ethnic allegiance for the moment. Many San Franciscans take up the offer. With so many pubs bearing names such as Harrington's, O'Keefe's, and McGowan's, there's plenty of free corned beef and cabbage, plus green beer and stirring Irish folk music. The St. Patrick's Day Parade draws participants as diverse as the Irish Wolfhounds of Sebastopol and the Twirl Girls of San Bruno. Like other ethnics, the Irish have their Grand Ball and their Miss Shamrock. But who else could muster some 70 snakes at Zellerbach Plaza, Market and Sansome, for a race recalling what St. Patrick might have done for the mother country if he had perchance existed.?

As an index of the city's internationalism, consider that Harold's Bookstore, 484 Geary, flies in foreign newspapers ranging from *Excelsior* of Mexico City to *Algemeine* of Frankfurt. Some 22 foreign language papers are produced in the San Francisco area, such as the French *Le Californien*. It has been argued that the proceedings of the United Nations would have been more fruitful if that organization could have stayed in San Francisco after its founding here in 1945.

The City That Encourages Innovation

San Francisco has always been a city that encouraged innovation in personal living, institutions, and architecture. When the innovation worked well, it quickly became a tradition. But the tradition was never seen as sacred. There was always room for the next innovator.

Take the Farmer's Market at 100 Alemany, near where highways 101-280 meet, as an example. In 1943 the gas and sugar shortages of World War II forced Bay Area canneries to cancel their pear contracts, so farmers brought their produce to San Francisco to sell it directly to the people. Apples, then vegetables, followed pears. Today the tradition persists, with 120 farmers from 41 California counties bringing some 78 commodities to this market without benefit of a middleman. Many of the crops are "organically" grown. The annual Spring Daffodil Festival in April on Maiden Lane, near Union Square, is another such tradition, an urban delight that caught on and was repeated.

There was a time when the best views of San Francisco were limited to three choices: the Top of the Mark, in the Mark Hopkins hotel; the Crown Room, in the Fairmont hotel; and the Starlight Roof at the Sir Francis Drake hotel. But then came the new downtown structures and their superlative platforms. The Carnelian Room of the Bank of America surpasses all competitors, placing you 52 stories above the town. Among the other new options, the Hyatt Regency's Equinox Room revolves, making a complete circle every 43 minutes.

San Francisco has always been a good place to listen to music. Through capable promoters, such as Bill Graham, San Francisco in the 1960s and '70s became a launching ground for hundreds of new rock groups, such as the Jefferson Airplane. But that didn't mean the city abandoned its symphony. Edo de Waart, the Dutchman who conducts the Rotterdam Philharmonic and has contracted to conduct the San Francisco Symphony into the early 1980s, remarked to me, "The breadth of community support for the symphony in San Francisco impresses me. In Rotterdam we have a more stratified Friends of the Orchestra. But in San Francisco, interest in symphony, with all the committeees, spreads much more widely throughout the community."

The ACT (American Conservatory Theater), launched in 1967, has firmly established itself at the Geary Theater, 415 Geary. And the Opera, performing now at the War Memorial-Opera House, has flourished since 1923.

Not only in music and theater, but in the plastic mediums, as well, there is a constant interplay between tradition and innovation. At one of the smart galleries, such as Bowles/Hopkins, 747 Beach, you can see elemental prints of the late Alexander Calder, but at the San Francisco Art Festival, a four-day outdoor show in late September, you can join some 400,000 viewers who flock to Civic Center for a look at current productions in a wide range of arts and crafts.

(Above:) The large campus of the University of California stretches below the towering campanile at Berkeley, in the East Bay Area.
(Below:) Framed by trees, south of San Francisco, Stanford University perpetuates the California Mission style of architecture.

(Above:) Following the trends in architecture, St. Mary's Cathedral is a showplace among the modern buildings in San Francisco.
(Below:) San Francisco is barely visible in the background here, in this view from Oakland's waterfront. A busy port, Oakland is the center for container shipping on the West Coast.

To some extent the city itself has always been regarded as a work of art, the city planner acting as artist, the buildings, open space, and amenities serving as the medium. The controversial innovation in the last decade has occurred in the downtown area of the 51-acre Golden Gateway development, west of Battery Street. These new buildings and their immediate surroundings are worth a walk, beginning at the Transamerica Pyramid, the refreshing building shape at Washington and Montgomery. The scale and daring of such new buildings pleases some San Franciscans and disturbs others, ("The Transamerica Pyramid would be OK if they'd just take it down after christmas."). A redwood grove planted next to the Pyramid has won wide acclaim as a brilliant spot of greenery amidst the stone, glass, and concrete.

At the end you descend toward the Hyatt Regency Hotel and the Justin Herman Plaza, a lively place for street artists, office workers taking a break, and urban joggers, all in front of the revered old Ferry Building with its clock and spire. On the Justin Herman Plaza stands the controversial Vaillancourt Fountain, 101 concrete boxes, a walk-through-the water participatory sculpture. To some San Franciscans the fountain is not regarded as a thing of beauty, but as a mocking approximation of the halted freeway overhead, ("Is this the fountain before or after the earthquake?").

San Francisco has always been in the forefront of lifestyle innovations. A milieu of personal freedom has been created through a mixture of tolerance and the anonymity of an urban area. One celebrated example of this that is now woven into the city's history is the saga of Emperor Norton. If there ever was a San Franciscan marching to a different drummer, it was Joshua Norton. He was an Englishman who came to San Francisco in 1849 at age 30 with $40,000 at his command, plus the skills required to parlay this sum into a qaurter-million-dollar fortune. At this point in his career Norton learned that his reach exceeded his grasp. While attempting to corner the rice market, he gambled everything and lost. Then Norton went into seclusion, emerging finally from his dark night of introspection a changed man, at least from his own perspective. He now believed he was Emperor Norton I. Fortunately, he had friends, was declared harmless, and was quickly raised to the status of city buffoon. As the emperor he wore an ornate military uniform, complete with sword, and marched about the city, faithfully attended by a retinue of his two favorite dogs, Bummer and Lazarus. He was allowed to "command" dinners gratis at local restaurants and to write small checks that the local banks honored in support of municipal comedy. Periodically he read proclamations reaffirming that he was indeed Emperor Norton I of the United States and Protector of Mexico. On occasion his proclamations ordered the dissolution of the Republican and Democratic parties in the interest of peace. When he died in 1880, the city gave him a sumptuous funeral.

To some degree Emperor Norton lives in the 20th century in all the cults and unusual lifestyles that San Francisco nourishes. The city is the center of the spiritual self-help and growth disciplines. Est, Arica, Silva Mind Control, Transcendental Meditation, Zen Buddhism, Rolfing, and Bio-energetics are but a few of the systems offered to the spiritual explorerer. Forty-year-old Werner Erhard directs Est programs in 25 cities from his office at 764 California. From his Erhard Seminars Training about 120,000 graduates have emerged after paying $300 to attempt a transformation of their experience of life.

70

A look at the phone book yellow pages under Religious Organizations reveals listings ranging from the Guru Bawa Fellowship to the Meher Baba League. The city has been a major starting point in the country for religious consciousness groups from the Orient. The most colorful annual expression of this is the peach cloth procession of the Hare Krishna enthusiasts every July 7 as they walk along John Kennedy Drive in Golden Gate Park on their way to the sea. At the Hare Krishna Ratheytra Jagannath Cart Festival and Procession you can see those top-notched, dancing, shave-headed cultists draw their carts by hand, re-enacting a 5,000-year-old Hindu custom, sending out clouds of their trademarked Spiritual Sky incense. Dressed in peach cloth, tennis shoes, and windbreakers if it's chilly, this mendicant sect dances along to their hypnotic chants, brass cymbals, and clay drums.

The Delancey Street Foundation is another unique San Francisco innovation. At the Delancey Street Restaurant, 2032 Union, your roast beef sandwich may be cooked by a former heroin addict and served by a waitress who is an ex-prostitute. In 1970 a creative man named John Maher managed to put together a small loan to form a non-profit organization where ex-addicts, failed prostitutes, and released cons could get a supportive start in the struggle for a better and more normal life. Maher managed to buy a home at 2563 Divisadero for the group and organized businesses in construction, restaurants, Christmas trees, plant and glassware, moving, auto repair, and movie extras. The last-mentioned enterprise is peculiar to San Francisco, where so many films are made. Maher specialized in providing large numbers of extras for crowd scenes. Not many observers of Delancey Street, as the organization was called, gave it much of a chance for survival, especially since it woud have to be self-supporting, generating its survival income through enterprises and donations, independent of any government financing. Delancey Street also committed itself to taking in whoever wished to join. Today the group flourishes, serving more than 350 people, meeting a monthly budget of $95,000.

And finally, where but in San Francisco can you see the Artist's Soap Box Derby? In the spring every three years (1978 next) the Museum of Modern Art sponsors this event. In the last competition, which took place on a steep road in McLaren Park, some 90 artists participated and 4,000 cheering fans attended. One artist's circular vehicle, studded with 12,000 pennies, was entitled ''Runaway Inflation''.

Steeped in history, yet modern and bustling — a city of constantly changing moods, sights, sounds and faces, we have depicted for you here *San Francisco* — showing some of its famous and not-so-famous (but equally gorgeous) scenes.

Immortalized in song and story, in moves and television programs, cosmopolitan, breathtakingly beautiful, and always exciting, we give you San Francisco — ''everybody's city''.

(Above:) *San Francisco, mecca for artists and the arts, is a good place to stage outdoor concerts. On a sunny Sunday morning at Union Square, fans listen to a rousing jazz session.*

(Below:) *Viewed from the Rockridge BART station at Oakland, the city of San Francisco again looks impressive. BART (Bay Area Rapid Transit) is the modern underground transit system for the city.*